Te__
Puppies

by Julie Peters

 HOUGHTON MIFFLIN   BOSTON

PHOTOGRAPHY CREDITS
Cover © Michael Newman/PhotoEdit
1 © Sonja Foos/ShutterStock **2** © Tom Rosenthal/SuperStock **3** © BIOS/Peter Arnold, Inc. **4** © Brian Sytnyk/ Masterfile **5** © Mark Bacon/Alamy **6** © Jim Zuckerman/CORBIS **7** © Sonja Foos/ShutterStock

Printed in China

ISBN 10: 0-618-88653-2
ISBN 13: 978-0-618-88653-1

3456789 0940 16 15 14 13 12 11
4500334673

Count the puppies 1 to 10.
Now hide three puppies
and count again.

How many puppies are left?

Eight hungry puppies love to eat.
Hide two puppies
from noses to feet.

Count how many puppies are left.   **3**

Seven puppies play in the hay.
Hide three little puppies
who are sleepy today.

How many are left?

Five puppies walk at the shore.
Hide three or four
or even more.

How many did you hide? How many are left?   **5**

Two little puppies nap in the sun.
Hide them both.
They had too much fun.

6 How many are left after you subtract 2?

One little puppy sits all alone.

There are no puppies to play with.

So he runs for home.

How many puppies are left?

Puppies at the Beach

Draw

Look at page 5. Draw an X for each black puppy you see. Draw a Y for each yellow puppy you see.

Tell About

Monitor/Clarify Look at page 5. Tell how many puppies are black. Tell how many puppies are yellow. Tell how many puppies there are in all.

Write

Look at page 5. Write how many puppies there are in all.